Alpha-Gal Allergy

A Beginner's Quick Start Overview and Guide to Managing the Condition Through Diet, with Sample Meat-Free Recipes and a 7-Day Meal Plan

mf

copyright © 2024 Patrick Marshwell

All rights reserved No part of this book may be reproduced, or stored in a retrieval system, or transmitted in any form or by any means, electronic, mechanical, photocopying, recording, or otherwise, without express written permission of the publisher.

Disclaimer

By reading this disclaimer, you are accepting the terms of the disclaimer in full. If you disagree with this disclaimer, please do not read the guide.

All of the content within this guide is provided for informational and educational purposes only, and should not be accepted as independent medical or other professional advice. The author is not a doctor, physician, nurse, mental health provider, or registered nutritionist/dietician. Therefore, using and reading this guide does not establish any form of a physician-patient relationship.

Always consult with a physician or another qualified health provider with any issues or questions you might have regarding any sort of medical condition. Do not ever disregard any qualified professional medical advice or delay seeking that advice because of anything you have read in this guide. The information in this guide is not intended to be any sort of medical advice and should not be used in lieu of any medical advice by a licensed and qualified medical professional.

The information in this guide has been compiled from a variety of known sources. However, the author cannot attest to or guarantee the accuracy of each source and thus should not be held liable for any errors or omissions.

You acknowledge that the publisher of this guide will not be held liable for any loss or damage of any kind incurred as a result of this guide or the reliance on any information provided within this guide. You acknowledge and agree that you assume all risk and responsibility for any action you undertake in response to the information in this guide.

Using this guide does not guarantee any particular result (e.g., weight loss or a cure). By reading this guide, you acknowledge that there are no guarantees to any specific outcome or results you can expect.

All product names, diet plans, or names used in this guide are for identification purposes only and are the property of their respective owners. The use of these names does not imply endorsement. All other trademarks cited herein are the property of their respective owners.

Where applicable, this guide is not intended to be a substitute for the original work of this diet plan and is, at most, a supplement to the original work for this diet plan and never a direct substitute. This guide is a personal expression of the facts of that diet plan.

Where applicable, persons shown in the cover images are stock photography models and the publisher has obtained the rights to use the images through license agreements with third-party stock image companies.

Table of Contents

Introduction   7
What Is Alpha-Gal Allergy?   9
   Symptoms   9
   Causes of Alpha-Gal Allergy   11
   Medical Treatments for Alpha-Gal Allergy   13
Natural Remedies for Alpha-Gal Allergy   16
   Probiotics   16
   Quercetin   19
   Herbal Antihistamines   23
   Vitamin C   25
   Omega-3 Fatty Acids   27
   Local Honey   29
   Green Tea   33
   Stress Management   39
   Avoidance of Triggers   43
Managing Alpha-Gal Through Diet   47
   Foods to Avoid   47
   Foods to Eat   51
7-Day Sample Meal Plan   54
   Tips for Making a Meal Plan   57
Sample Recipes   59
   Overnight Oats   60
   Hummus and Veggie Wrap   62
   Lentil Curry Over Quinoa   64
   Tofu Scramble with Veggies and Whole Wheat Toast   67
   Black Bean and Corn Salad with Avocado on Mixed Greens   69
   Baked Sweet Potato Topped   70
   Smoothie Made with Banana, Spinach, Almond Milk, and Chia Seeds   72

Quinoa Veggie Bowl Topped with Tempeh and Tahini Dressing 73

Cauliflower Steak with Roasted Vegetables and Brown Rice 76

Oatmeal Topped with Almond Milk, Sliced Banana, and a Sprinkle of Cinnamon 79

Veggie Burger on Whole Wheat Bun with Tomato, Lettuce, and Avocado Spread 81

Stir Fry Made with Tofu, Mixed Vegetables, and Brown Rice 83

Avocado Toast Topped with Cherry Tomatoes and Balsamic Glaze 85

Quinoa Salad with Roasted Vegetables, Chickpeas, and a Lemon Vinaigrette Dressing 87

Vegan Chili Served Over Sweet Potato Noodles 90

Conclusion **92**

FAQs **96**

References and Helpful Links **99**

Introduction

Alpha-Gal Allergy, an emerging condition, has garnered increased attention in recent years. Triggered by the bite of the Lone Star tick, this allergy necessitates significant lifestyle adjustments for those affected. Understanding and managing Alpha-Gal Allergy can feel daunting, but with the right guidance and resources, it is possible to live a fulfilling life despite its challenges.

This management guide serves as an invaluable resource for anyone navigating the complexities of Alpha-Gal Allergy. It offers practical advice and strategies to help individuals adapt to their new circumstances. The focus is on empowering readers with supportive, informative content that enables them to take control of their health and well-being.

Living with Alpha-Gal Allergy involves more than just dietary changes; it requires a shift in lifestyle and mindset. Every decision, from food selections to social interactions, demands careful consideration and adaptation.

In this guide, we will talk about the following:

- What is Alpha-Gal Allergy?
- Natural Remedies for Alpha-Gal Allergy
- Managing Alpha-Gal Through Diet
- Foods to Avoid and Tom Eat
- 7-Day Sample Meal Plan
- Sample Recipes

By fostering a deep understanding and offering a wealth of practical knowledge, this guide acts as a companion on the journey with Alpha-Gal Allergy. It extends beyond being a mere collection of information, becoming a source of encouragement and support. Through shared experiences and collective wisdom, individuals can find new ways to thrive and enjoy life, despite the challenges posed by this condition.

What Is Alpha-Gal Allergy?

Alpha-gal allergy was first identified in the late 2000s by researchers studying cases of anaphylaxis in individuals living near Lone Star ticks (Amblyomma americanum) in the United States. These individuals exhibited symptoms of severe allergic reactions after consuming red meat, which led to further investigations into the connection between tick bites and mammalian meat allergies.

Ticks are known to carry a variety of microorganisms that can be transmitted to humans through their bites. It is believed that lone star tick bites trigger the development of alpha-gal allergy by introducing alpha-gal molecules into the human body, causing an immune response and the production of antibodies. These antibodies then cause an allergic reaction when exposed to mammalian meat containing alpha-gal.

Symptoms

The most common symptom of alpha-gal allergy is an allergic reaction after consuming mammalian meats. These reactions can range from mild to severe and may include:

1. ***Hives or Rash***: Itchy, red welts on the skin that can appear anywhere on the body. These are often the first signs of an allergic reaction.
2. ***Swelling***: This can occur in various parts of the body, including the lips, face, tongue, and throat, potentially leading to difficulty breathing.
3. ***Stomach Pain***: Abdominal discomfort, cramping, or pain, often accompanied by nausea or vomiting.
4. ***Diarrhea***: Frequent, loose, or watery bowel movements, which can be a sign of gastrointestinal distress.
5. ***Shortness of Breath***: Difficulty breathing or a feeling of tightness in the chest, which can be a serious symptom requiring immediate medical attention.
6. ***Headaches***: Persistent or severe headaches that can occur as part of the allergic reaction.
7. ***Runny Nose***: Nasal congestion or a runny nose, similar to symptoms of hay fever or other allergies.
8. ***Sneezing***: Frequent sneezing fits, often accompanied by a runny or stuffy nose.
9. ***Anaphylaxis***: A severe, potentially life-threatening allergic reaction that can cause a rapid drop in blood pressure, loss of consciousness, and difficulty breathing. This requires immediate emergency treatment.

10. *Fatigue*: Unusual tiredness or exhaustion that can occur after consuming red meat or other products containing alpha-gal.
11. *Dizziness or Fainting*: Feeling lightheaded or faint, which can be a sign of a severe allergic reaction.
12. *Heartburn or Indigestion*: A burning sensation in the chest or discomfort in the upper abdomen, often mistaken for other digestive issues.

If you experience any of these symptoms after consuming red meat or products containing alpha-gal, it is important to seek medical attention. While some reactions may be mild, others can be severe and potentially life-threatening. It is also important to inform your doctor or allergist about your potential allergy to alpha-gal so they can make appropriate recommendations for treatment and avoidance.

Causes of Alpha-Gal Allergy

The following are some possible causes of alpha-gal allergy:

1. *Tick Bites*: The primary cause of Alpha-Gal Allergy is bites from certain types of ticks, particularly the Lone Star tick in the United States. When these ticks bite humans, they can transfer alpha-gal (a sugar molecule found in most mammals) into the bloodstream, triggering an immune response.
2. *Immune System Reaction*: After a tick bite, the immune system may start to recognize alpha-gal as a

threat. This leads to the production of specific antibodies (IgE) against alpha-gal, which can cause allergic reactions when red meat or other products containing alpha-gal are consumed.

3. **Consumption of Mammalian Meat**: Eating red meat (such as beef, pork, lamb, and venison) or other mammalian products (like gelatin or dairy) can trigger allergic reactions in individuals sensitized to alpha-gal. The symptoms often appear several hours after consumption.
4. **Exposure to Alpha-Gal in Medications**: Some medications and medical products contain alpha-gal, which can also trigger allergic reactions in sensitized individuals. This includes certain vaccines, biological drugs, and gelatin-based capsules.
5. **Geographic Location**: Living in or traveling to areas where the Lone Star tick or other alpha-gal-carrying ticks are prevalent increases the risk of developing Alpha-Gal Allergy. These areas include the southeastern and eastern United States, as well as parts of Europe, Australia, and Asia.
6. **Outdoor Activities**: Engaging in outdoor activities such as hiking, camping, or hunting in tick-infested areas increases the likelihood of tick bites, thereby raising the risk of developing Alpha-Gal Allergy.
7. **Lack of Awareness and Prevention**: Not taking preventive measures against tick bites, such as using

insect repellent, wearing protective clothing, and performing regular tick checks, can increase the risk of being bitten by ticks that carry alpha-gal.

Understanding these causes can help in taking preventive measures and managing the allergy effectively. If you suspect you have Alpha-Gal Allergy, it's important to seek medical advice for proper diagnosis and treatment.

Medical Treatments for Alpha-Gal Allergy

Currently, there is no cure for Alpha-Gal Allergy. However, there are various medical treatments that can help manage the symptoms and prevent severe reactions. These include:

1. *Antihistamines*: These medications can help relieve mild to moderate allergic symptoms such as hives, itching, and runny nose. They work by blocking the action of histamine, a substance in the body that causes allergic symptoms.
2. *Epinephrine Auto-Injectors*: For severe allergic reactions (anaphylaxis), carrying an epinephrine auto-injector (such as an EpiPen) is crucial. Epinephrine can quickly reverse the symptoms of anaphylaxis, including difficulty breathing and swelling.
3. *Avoidance of Red Meat and Mammalian Products*: The most effective way to manage Alpha-Gal Allergy is to avoid consuming red meat and other mammalian

products that contain alpha-gal. This includes beef, pork, lamb, venison, and certain dairy products.
4. **_Dietary Counseling_**: Working with a dietitian or nutritionist can help individuals with Alpha-Gal Allergy identify safe foods and create a balanced diet that avoids alpha-gal-containing products.
5. **_Allergy Medications_**: In some cases, doctors may prescribe corticosteroids or other allergy medications to manage symptoms and reduce inflammation.
6. **_Monitoring and Follow-Up_**: Regular follow-up appointments with an allergist or healthcare provider are important to monitor the condition, adjust treatment plans, and ensure that the allergy is being managed effectively.
7. **_Education and Awareness_**: Educating patients and their families about the allergy, its triggers, and how to avoid them is a key component of managing Alpha-Gal Allergy. This includes understanding food labels and being aware of hidden sources of alpha-gal.
8. **_Emergency Action Plan_**: Having a personalized emergency action plan in place can help individuals and their families know what to do in case of a severe allergic reaction. This plan should include the use of epinephrine and when to seek emergency medical help.

These treatments can help manage the symptoms and reduce the risk of severe allergic reactions. If you suspect you have Alpha-Gal Allergy, it's important to consult with a healthcare professional for proper diagnosis and treatment.

Natural Remedies for Alpha-Gal Allergy

In this chapter, we will discuss some natural remedies that may help alleviate the symptoms of Alpha-Gal Allergy. It's important to note that these remedies have not been scientifically proven to cure or treat the allergy, and should always be used in conjunction with medical treatment.

Probiotics

Probiotics, which are live bacteria and yeast, play a crucial role in maintaining digestive health. Emerging research suggests that these beneficial microorganisms may also help reduce the severity of allergic reactions, including those associated with Alpha-Gal Allergy, by improving gut health and immune function.

How Probiotics Improve Digestive Health

Probiotics help balance the gut microbiome, the complex community of microorganisms living in the digestive tract. A healthy gut microbiome is essential for:

- ***Digestive Efficiency***: Probiotics enhance the breakdown and absorption of nutrients.
- ***Barrier Function***: They strengthen the gut lining, preventing harmful substances from entering the bloodstream.
- ***Inflammation Reduction***: They help regulate inflammatory responses, which can be beneficial in managing allergies.

Probiotics and Allergic Reactions

Probiotics can help modulate the immune system, potentially reducing the severity of allergic reactions. Here's how:

- ***Immune Modulation***: Certain probiotic strains can help balance the immune response, reducing hypersensitivity to allergens.
- ***Anti-Inflammatory Effects***: Probiotics produce short-chain fatty acids (SCFAs) that have anti-inflammatory properties, which may alleviate allergic symptoms.
- ***Gut Health***: A healthy gut microbiome can prevent dysbiosis (microbial imbalance), which is often linked to increased allergic reactions.

Beneficial Probiotic Strains

Not all probiotics are the same; specific strains have been identified for their potential benefits in allergy management:

- ***Lactobacillus rhamnosus GG (LGG)***: Known for its ability to enhance gut barrier function and modulate immune responses.
- ***Bifidobacterium lactis***: Helps reduce intestinal inflammation and supports overall gut health.
- ***Lactobacillus acidophilus***: Aids in maintaining a balanced gut microbiome and has been shown to reduce the severity of allergic reactions.
- ***Bifidobacterium longum***: Known for its immune-modulating properties, which can help reduce allergic symptoms.

Natural Sources of Probiotics

Incorporating natural sources of probiotics into your diet can help maintain a healthy gut microbiome:

- *Yogurt*: Opt for dairy-free versions made from almond, soy, or coconut milk to avoid alpha-gal.
- *Kefir*: A fermented drink available as a plant-based alternative.
- *Sauerkraut*: Fermented cabbage rich in probiotics.
- *Kimchi*: A spicy Korean dish made from fermented vegetables.
- *Tempeh*: A fermented soybean product that's an excellent source of probiotics and protein.
- *Miso*: A fermented soybean paste used in soups and dishes.

The Importance of a Healthy Gut Microbiome

Maintaining a healthy gut microbiome is vital for overall health and can be particularly beneficial for individuals with Alpha-Gal Allergy. Here's why:

- *Digestive Health*: A balanced gut microbiome improves digestion and nutrient absorption.
- *Immune Function*: A healthy microbiome supports a robust immune system, reducing the likelihood of severe allergic reactions.
- *Mental Health*: Emerging research suggests a link between gut health and mental well-being, highlighting the importance of a balanced microbiome for overall health.

Incorporating probiotics into your diet, either through natural sources or supplements, can be a beneficial strategy for managing Alpha-Gal Allergy. By supporting gut health and modulating the immune response, probiotics offer a promising approach to reducing the severity of allergic reactions and enhancing overall well-being.

Quercetin

Quercetin is a powerful plant compound known for its antioxidant and anti-inflammatory properties, making it a valuable addition to the diet of individuals with Alpha-Gal Allergy. Found in various fruits, vegetables, and herbs, quercetin can help alleviate allergic reactions and support overall health.

Role as an Antioxidant

As an antioxidant, quercetin helps protect the body from oxidative stress caused by free radicals. Oxidative stress can damage cells and contribute to inflammation, which is particularly relevant for individuals with Alpha-Gal Allergy. By neutralizing free radicals, quercetin helps:

- *Prevent Cellular Damage*: Protects cells from oxidative damage and maintains cellular integrity.
- *Reduce Inflammation*: Lowers the risk of chronic inflammation, which can exacerbate allergic reactions.
- *Support Immune Health*: Enhances immune function by protecting immune cells from oxidative stress.

Anti-Inflammatory Properties

Quercetin's anti-inflammatory effects are particularly beneficial for managing allergic reactions. Here's how it works:

- *Inhibition of Inflammatory Pathways*: Quercetin blocks the release of histamines, compounds responsible for allergic symptoms like itching, swelling, and redness.
- *Reduction of Eicosanoid Production*: Eicosanoids are signaling molecules that play a key role in

inflammation. Quercetin inhibits their production, thereby reducing inflammation.
- *Modulation of Immune Responses*: Quercetin can help balance the immune system, making it less reactive to allergens.

Benefits for Individuals with Alpha-Gal Allergy

For those with Alpha-Gal Allergy, quercetin offers several specific benefits:

- *Symptom Relief*: By reducing the release of histamines and other inflammatory mediators, quercetin can help alleviate symptoms such as hives, itching, and gastrointestinal distress.
- *Enhanced Immune Function*: Quercetin supports a balanced immune system, reducing the severity and frequency of allergic reactions.
- *Gut Health*: Its anti-inflammatory properties can help maintain a healthy gut lining, preventing leaky gut syndrome, which is often linked to increased allergic sensitivity.

Natural Sources of Quercetin

Incorporating quercetin-rich foods into your diet is a natural way to harness its benefits. Here are some excellent sources:

- *Fruits*: Apples, berries (especially cranberries and blueberries), grapes, and citrus fruits.

- *Vegetables*: Onions (especially red onions), broccoli, kale, and bell peppers.
- *Herbs*: Parsley, cilantro, and dill.
- *Other Sources*: Green tea, red wine, and capers.

Research Findings

Research on quercetin highlights its potential in managing allergies and inflammation. Some relevant findings include:

- *Histamine Inhibition*: Studies have shown that quercetin can inhibit histamine release from mast cells, reducing allergic reactions.
- *Anti-Inflammatory Effects*: Research indicates that quercetin can lower the production of pro-inflammatory cytokines, molecules that promote inflammation.
- *Immune Modulation*: Evidence suggests that quercetin can help modulate the immune system, making it less likely to overreact to allergens.

Incorporating quercetin-rich foods into your diet or considering quercetin supplements (after consulting with a healthcare provider) can be a beneficial strategy for managing Alpha-Gal Allergy. Its antioxidant and anti-inflammatory properties offer a natural way to reduce the severity of allergic reactions and support overall health.

Herbal Antihistamines

Herbal antihistamines are gaining attention for their potential to alleviate allergic reactions naturally. Certain herbs, such as stinging nettle, butterbur, and quercetin, are known for their antihistamine properties, which can be particularly beneficial for individuals with Alpha-Gal Allergy. Here's an in-depth look at these herbs, their benefits, and how they can be incorporated into your wellness routine.

Stinging Nettle (Urtica dioica)

Stinging nettle is a herb traditionally used for its anti-inflammatory and antihistamine properties. Research suggests that it may help reduce allergic reactions by inhibiting the production of histamines and other inflammatory mediators.

- *How It Works*: Stinging nettle contains compounds that can block histamine receptors, reducing the release of histamines and alleviating symptoms like itching, swelling, and congestion.
- *Benefits*: In addition to its antihistamine effects, stinging nettle is rich in vitamins A and C, iron, and potassium, supporting overall health and immune function.
- *How to Consume*: Stinging nettle can be taken as a supplement in capsule or tablet form, or as a tea. Fresh

or dried nettle leaves can also be added to soups and salads.

Butterbur (Petasites hybridus)

Butterbur is another herb known for its anti-inflammatory and antihistamine properties. It has been used for centuries to treat allergies and respiratory conditions.

- *How It Works*: Butterbur contains petasin and isopetasin, compounds that inhibit leukotrienes and histamines, reducing inflammation and allergic symptoms.
- *Benefits*: Besides its antihistamine effects, butterbur may help relieve migraines and support respiratory health.
- *How to Consume*: Butterbur is typically taken as a capsule or tablet supplement. It's important to choose butterbur products labeled "PA-free" to avoid compounds that can cause liver damage.

Incorporating these natural remedies into your allergy management plan may help provide relief and reduce the need for medications with potential side effects. However, it's always best to consult with a healthcare professional before starting any new supplements or herbal treatments.

Vitamin C

Vitamin C, also known as ascorbic acid, is renowned for its natural antihistamine properties, making it a valuable nutrient for individuals with Alpha-Gal Allergy. This essential vitamin not only supports immune function but also helps reduce the severity of allergic reactions, providing a natural way to manage allergy symptoms.

Natural Antihistamine Properties

Vitamin C acts as a natural antihistamine by:

- ***Reducing Histamine Levels***: It helps break down histamine, a compound released during allergic reactions, thereby reducing symptoms such as itching, swelling, and congestion.
- ***Inhibiting Histamine Release***: Vitamin C can prevent mast cells from releasing histamines, lowering the overall allergic response.
- ***Anti-Inflammatory Effects***: It reduces inflammation associated with allergic reactions, helping to alleviate symptoms and improve overall comfort.

Benefits for Individuals with Alpha-Gal Allergy

For those dealing with Alpha-Gal Allergy, vitamin C offers several specific benefits:

- ***Symptom Relief***: By reducing histamine levels and preventing its release, vitamin C can help mitigate

symptoms such as hives, itching, and gastrointestinal distress.
- ***Immune Support***: Vitamin C enhances the function of immune cells, helping to maintain a balanced immune response that is less prone to overreacting to allergens.
- ***Antioxidant Protection***: It protects cells from oxidative stress caused by free radicals, which can exacerbate inflammation and allergic reactions.

Natural Sources of Vitamin C

Incorporating vitamin C-rich foods into your diet is a natural way to benefit from its antihistamine properties. Here are some excellent sources:

- ***Citrus Fruits***: Oranges, lemons, limes, grapefruits, and tangerines.
- ***Berries***: Strawberries, blueberries, raspberries, and blackberries.
- ***Bell Peppers***: Red, green, yellow, and orange bell peppers.
- ***Cruciferous Vegetables***: Broccoli, Brussels sprouts, and kale.
- ***Other Sources***: Kiwi, pineapple, mango, and tomatoes.

Incorporating vitamin C into your daily routine, either through diet or supplements (after consulting with a healthcare provider), can be a beneficial strategy for managing Alpha Gal Allergy. By leveraging its natural antihistamine and immune-boosting properties, vitamin C offers a safe and effective way to reduce the severity of allergic reactions and support overall health.

Omega-3 Fatty Acids

Omega-3 fatty acids are essential fats known for their potent anti-inflammatory properties. These beneficial fats, found in sources such as fish oil, flaxseeds, and walnuts, can play a crucial role in reducing allergic symptoms, making them a valuable addition to the diet of individuals with Alpha-Gal Allergy.

Anti-Inflammatory Properties

Omega-3 fatty acids help reduce inflammation in the body, which is particularly beneficial for managing allergic reactions. Here's how they work:

- Inhibition of Inflammatory Pathways: Omega-3s reduce the production of inflammatory cytokines and eicosanoids, which are signaling molecules that contribute to inflammation and allergic responses.
- Cell Membrane Health: They improve the fluidity and function of cell membranes, enhancing the overall health and responsiveness of cells involved in the immune response.
- Balancing Omega-6 Fatty Acids: Omega-3s help balance the intake of omega-6 fatty acids, which are

often more prevalent in modern diets and can promote inflammation when consumed in excess.

Benefits for Individuals with Alpha-Gal Allergy

For those with Alpha-Gal Allergy, omega-3 fatty acids offer several specific benefits:

- *Symptom Relief*: By reducing inflammation and modulating immune responses, omega-3s can help alleviate symptoms such as hives, itching, and gastrointestinal discomfort.
- *Immune System Support*: Omega-3s enhance the function of immune cells, promoting a more balanced and less reactive immune system.
- *Heart Health*: They support cardiovascular health, which can be beneficial since chronic inflammation is a risk factor for heart disease.

Natural Sources of Omega-3 Fatty Acids

Incorporating omega-3-rich foods into your diet is an effective way to harness their benefits. Here are some excellent sources:

- *Fish and Seafood*: Fatty fish such as salmon, mackerel, sardines, and anchovies are rich in EPA and DHA, the most bioavailable forms of omega-3s.

- ***Plant-Based Sources***: Flaxseeds, chia seeds, hemp seeds, and walnuts are good sources of ALA, a plant-based omega-3 fatty acid.
- ***Oils***: Flaxseed oil, walnut oil, and canola oil are also high in ALA.

Incorporating omega-3 fatty acids into your diet, either through food or supplements (after consulting with a healthcare provider), can be a beneficial strategy for managing Alpha-Gal Allergy. Their anti-inflammatory and immune-modulating properties offer a natural way to reduce the severity of allergic reactions and support overall health.

Local Honey

Local honey has been touted by many as a natural remedy for allergies. The idea is that consuming honey produced by bees in your local area can help build immunity to local allergens, potentially easing allergy symptoms. While scientific evidence supporting this theory is limited, many anecdotal reports suggest that local honey can provide some relief for mild allergy symptoms.

The Theory Behind Local Honey and Immunity

The concept is similar to the principle behind allergy shots (immunotherapy). Bees collect pollen from local plants, which is then incorporated into the honey they produce. By consuming small amounts of this honey regularly, the theory is that your body becomes gradually desensitized to the pollen, reducing the severity of allergic reactions over time. Here's how it is believed to work:

- ***Exposure to Allergens***: Regular consumption of local honey exposes your body to small amounts of the allergens present in the pollen.
- ***Immune Response Modulation***: This exposure is thought to help your immune system recognize and become less reactive to these allergens, potentially reducing allergic symptoms.

Potential Benefits for Mild Allergy Symptoms

While the scientific community remains skeptical due to a lack of robust evidence, some people report experiencing relief from mild allergy symptoms after consuming local honey. The potential benefits include:

- ***Reduction in Symptoms***: Some individuals find that their symptoms, such as sneezing, runny nose, and itchy eyes, are less severe when they regularly consume local honey.
- ***Natural Remedy***: For those seeking natural alternatives to conventional antihistamines, local honey offers a potentially soothing option.

Scientific Evidence and Limitations

The scientific evidence supporting the use of local honey for allergy relief is limited and mixed. Several studies have been conducted, but their findings are not conclusive:

- *Positive Anecdotal Reports*: Many people swear by the effectiveness of local honey for their allergy symptoms, attributing their relief to regular consumption.
- *Mixed Research Findings*: Some studies have found slight improvements in allergy symptoms, while others have found no significant difference compared to a placebo.
- *Placebo Effect*: It's possible that the benefits some people experience from consuming local honey are due to the placebo effect, where belief in the treatment's efficacy contributes to perceived improvement.

How to Incorporate Local Honey into Your Diet

If you're interested in trying local honey for allergy relief, here are some ways to incorporate it into your diet:

- *Daily Spoonful*: Take a teaspoon of local honey each day, either on its own or mixed into a beverage.
- *Sweeten Foods*: Use local honey as a natural sweetener in tea, coffee, yogurt, oatmeal, and smoothies.

- *Baking and Cooking*: Substitute sugar with local honey in baking or drizzle it over toast, pancakes, or fruit.

Safety Considerations

While local honey is generally safe for most people, there are some important considerations to keep in mind:

- *Allergic Reactions*: If you have a severe allergy to pollen or bee products, consuming local honey may trigger an allergic reaction. Consult with a healthcare provider before trying it.
- *Infants*: Honey should not be given to infants under one year of age due to the risk of botulism, a rare but serious form of food poisoning.
- *Moderation*: Honey is high in natural sugars and calories, so it should be consumed in moderation as part of a balanced diet.

In summary, while scientific evidence supporting the use of local honey for allergy relief is inconclusive, many people find it helpful for managing mild symptoms. By incorporating local honey into your diet responsibly, you may experience some of these potential benefits. Always consult with a healthcare provider before starting any new treatment to ensure it is safe and appropriate for your individual health needs.

Green Tea

Green tea, a popular beverage known for its numerous health benefits, is rich in antioxidants and has potential mild antihistamine effects. These properties can help boost the immune system and may provide relief for individuals with Alpha-Gal Allergy. Understanding how green tea can aid in managing allergy symptoms can be valuable for those seeking natural remedies.

Antioxidant Properties

Green tea is packed with antioxidants, particularly catechins, and polyphenols, which play a crucial role in neutralizing free radicals and reducing oxidative stress in the body. These antioxidants offer several benefits:

- *Cell Protection*: Antioxidants protect cells from damage caused by free radicals, which can exacerbate inflammation and allergic reactions.
- *Anti-Inflammatory Effects*: By reducing oxidative stress, green tea helps lower inflammation, a common issue for individuals with allergies.
- *Immune System Support*: Antioxidants support the immune system, helping it function more effectively and reducing the likelihood of overreacting to allergens.

Boosting the Immune System

A healthy immune system is key to managing allergies effectively. Green tea contributes to immune health in several ways:

- ***Enhancing Immune Function***: The polyphenols in green tea, especially epigallocatechin gallate (EGCG), have been shown to enhance the activity of immune cells, improving the body's ability to fend off infections and respond to allergens appropriately.
- ***Balancing Immune Responses***: Green tea can help regulate the immune system, promoting a balanced response that is less prone to the exaggerated reactions seen in allergic responses.

Mild Antihistamine Effects

Green tea may also act as a mild antihistamine, providing additional relief for allergy sufferers:

- ***Inhibition of Histamine Release***: Some studies suggest that green tea can inhibit the release of histamines from mast cells, reducing symptoms such as itching, swelling, and congestion.
- ***Symptom Relief***: By lowering histamine levels, green tea can help alleviate common allergy symptoms, making it a useful addition to an allergy management plan.

Benefits for Individuals with Alpha-Gal Allergy

For those with Alpha-Gal Allergy, green tea offers specific benefits:

- *Symptom Management*: The antihistamine and anti-inflammatory properties of green tea can help reduce the severity of reactions to alpha-gal, a carbohydrate found in red meat that triggers allergic responses.
- *Immune Support*: By boosting immune function, green tea helps maintain a balanced immune system, which is crucial for managing allergies effectively.
- *Overall Health*: Regular consumption of green tea contributes to overall health and well-being, supporting various bodily functions that can be impacted by chronic inflammation and allergic reactions.

How to Incorporate Green Tea into Your Diet

Incorporating green tea into your daily routine is easy and can be done in several ways:

- *Hot or Iced Tea*: Enjoy green tea hot or iced, with or without natural sweeteners like honey or lemon.
- *Green Tea Extract*: Consider using green tea extracts or supplements, but consult with a healthcare provider first to determine the appropriate dosage.

- ***Cooking and Baking***: Use green tea powder (matcha) in cooking and baking, adding it to smoothies, desserts, and other recipes for a nutritional boost.

Green tea is a beneficial addition to the diet of individuals with Alpha-Gal Allergy. Its antioxidant, immune-boosting, and mild antihistamine properties offer a natural way to reduce the severity of allergic reactions and support overall health. As with any new treatment, it is advisable to consult with a healthcare provider to ensure it is suitable for your individual health needs.

Hydration

Staying well-hydrated is a fundamental aspect of overall health and can significantly impact the management of allergy symptoms, including those associated with Alpha-Gal Allergy. Proper hydration helps thin mucus and reduce congestion, providing relief from some of the most bothersome symptoms. Understanding the role of hydration and implementing strategies to stay adequately hydrated can offer substantial benefits for those dealing with allergies.

How Hydration Helps with Allergy Symptoms

Hydration plays a crucial role in maintaining the body's natural defense mechanisms against allergens. Here's how it works:

- ***Thinning Mucus***: Adequate hydration helps to thin mucus, making it easier to expel from the body. This can reduce nasal congestion and sinus pressure, which are common symptoms of allergies.
- ***Reducing Congestion***: By keeping the mucous membranes moist, hydration helps maintain their integrity and functionality, reducing the likelihood of congestion and facilitating easier breathing.
- ***Supporting Immune Function***: Water is essential for the proper functioning of the immune system. It helps transport nutrients to cells and remove toxins, supporting overall immune health and reducing the severity of allergic reactions.

Specific Benefits for Individuals with Alpha-Gal Allergy

For those with Alpha-Gal Allergy, staying hydrated offers several specific advantages:

- ***Symptom Relief***: Hydration can help alleviate symptoms such as nasal congestion, sinus pressure, and throat irritation, which can be exacerbated by allergic reactions to alpha-gal.
- ***Digestive Health***: Proper hydration supports the digestive system, which can be beneficial for managing gastrointestinal symptoms sometimes associated with Alpha-Gal Allergy.
- ***Overall Well-being***: Adequate water intake contributes to overall physical well-being, which is particularly

important for individuals dealing with chronic allergic conditions.

Importance of Hydration

Maintaining proper hydration is vital for numerous bodily functions, including:

- *Regulating Body Temperature*: Water helps regulate body temperature through sweating and respiration, which is essential during physical activity and in hot environments.
- *Joint and Muscle Function*: Hydration supports joint lubrication and muscle function, reducing the risk of cramps and injuries.
- *Skin Health*: Well-hydrated skin is more resilient and less prone to irritation and dryness, which can be aggravated by allergic reactions.

Tips for Staying Hydrated

Incorporating simple strategies into your daily routine can help you maintain optimal hydration levels:

- *Drink Regularly*: Sip water throughout the day rather than waiting until you're thirsty, as thirst is often a sign that you're already becoming dehydrated.
- *Carry a Water Bottle*: Keep a reusable water bottle with you to make it easy to drink water on the go.

- ***Eat Hydrating Foods***: Include fruits and vegetables with high water content in your diet, such as cucumbers, watermelon, oranges, and strawberries.
- ***Set Reminders***: Use alarms or apps to remind yourself to drink water at regular intervals, especially if you have a busy schedule.
- ***Monitor Urine Color***: Aim for light yellow urine, which is a good indicator of proper hydration.

Staying well-hydrated is a simple yet effective way to manage allergy symptoms, including Alpha-Gal Allergy. Proper hydration can thin mucus, reduce congestion, and support immune function, making a noticeable difference in your comfort. Incorporate these hydration tips into your daily routine to help manage allergy symptoms and maintain good health. Always consult a healthcare provider for personalized advice on your specific health needs.

Stress Management

Managing stress is essential for overall health, especially for those with chronic conditions like Alpha-Gal Allergy. Practices such as yoga, meditation, and deep-breathing exercises can significantly reduce stress, helping to manage allergic reactions. Recognizing the link between stress and allergy symptoms, along with the benefits of stress management, offers valuable insights for those seeking natural ways to ease their symptoms.

The Connection Between Stress and Allergy Symptoms

Stress has a profound impact on the body's immune system and can exacerbate allergic reactions. Here's how stress influences allergy symptoms:

- *Immune System Suppression*: Chronic stress can suppress the immune system, making it less efficient at dealing with allergens and increasing the severity of allergic reactions.
- *Inflammatory Response*: Stress triggers the release of stress hormones such as cortisol, which can increase inflammation in the body, worsening allergy symptoms.
- *Histamine Release*: Stress can prompt the body to release more histamine, a chemical involved in allergic reactions, leading to heightened symptoms such as itching, swelling, and congestion.

Benefits for Individuals with Alpha-Gal Allergy

For those with Alpha-Gal Allergy, managing stress can offer several specific benefits:

- *Symptom Reduction*: By lowering stress levels, individuals may experience a reduction in the severity and frequency of allergic reactions to alpha-gal, a carbohydrate found in red meat.

- ***Improved Immune Function***: Stress management helps strengthen the immune system, enabling it to respond more appropriately to allergens.
- ***Enhanced Overall Health***: Reducing stress contributes to better overall health, which is particularly important for individuals managing chronic allergic conditions.

Effective Stress Management Practices

Incorporating stress management practices into daily life can help alleviate allergy symptoms. Here are some effective techniques:

- *Yoga*: Yoga combines physical postures, breathing exercises, and meditation to promote relaxation and reduce stress. Regular practice can help lower cortisol levels, improve flexibility, and enhance mental clarity.
- *Meditation*: Meditation involves focusing the mind and eliminating distractions to achieve a state of calm and relaxation. It can reduce anxiety, lower blood pressure, and improve overall emotional well-being.
- *Deep-Breathing Exercises*: Deep breathing helps activate the body's relaxation response, reducing stress and promoting a sense of calm. Techniques such as diaphragmatic breathing and alternate nostril breathing can be particularly effective.

Tips for Incorporating Stress Management Practices into Daily Life

Integrating stress management practices into your daily routine can be simple and beneficial. Here are some tips:

- *Set Aside Time*: Dedicate specific times each day for stress management activities, even if it's just 10-15 minutes. Consistency is key to reaping the benefits.
- *Create a Relaxing Space*: Designate a quiet, comfortable area in your home for yoga, meditation, or deep-breathing exercises. This space should be free from distractions.
- *Start Small*: If you're new to stress management practices, start with short sessions and gradually increase the duration as you become more comfortable.
- *Use Guided Resources*: Take advantage of guided yoga classes, meditation apps, or online tutorials to help you learn and stay motivated.
- *Combine Techniques*: Experiment with combining different stress management techniques to find what works best for you. For example, you might start with deep breathing exercises before moving into a meditation session.

Managing stress through practices like yoga, meditation, and deep-breathing exercises can significantly reduce the severity of allergic reactions associated with Alpha-Gal Allergy. By understanding the connection between stress and allergy symptoms, individuals can take proactive steps to incorporate stress management techniques into their daily lives.

These practices not only help alleviate allergy symptoms but also contribute to overall physical and emotional well-being. Always consult with a healthcare provider to ensure that these practices are suitable for your specific health needs.

Avoidance of Triggers

When it comes to managing Alpha-Gal Allergy, avoidance of known triggers is paramount. This includes steering clear of red meat and mammalian products, as well as being vigilant about food labels and potential cross-contamination. Understanding the importance of these precautions and implementing effective strategies can significantly reduce the risk of allergic reactions and enhance the quality of life for those affected by this condition.

Importance of Avoiding Known Triggers

For individuals with Alpha-Gal Allergy, exposure to alpha-gal, a carbohydrate found in red meat and other mammalian products, can trigger severe allergic reactions. These reactions can range from mild symptoms such as hives and gastrointestinal distress to more severe manifestations like anaphylaxis. Therefore, strict avoidance of known triggers is essential to prevent these adverse health outcomes:

- ***Red Meat***: This includes beef, pork, lamb, and other meats derived from mammals.
- ***Mammalian Products***: Gelatin, dairy products, and certain medications or supplements that might contain mammalian derivatives.

Vigilance About Food Labels and Cross-Contamination

Reading food labels meticulously and being aware of cross-contamination risks are critical steps in managing Alpha-Gal Allergy:

- ***Food Labels***: Always check ingredient lists for hidden sources of mammalian products. Be cautious with processed foods, as they may contain gelatin or other mammalian-derived ingredients.
- ***Cross-Contamination***: Be aware of the potential for cross-contamination in kitchens, restaurants, and food processing facilities. Use separate utensils and cookware to avoid accidental exposure.

Tips for Effectively Avoiding Triggers

Implementing practical strategies can help individuals with Alpha-Gal Allergy navigate their daily lives more safely:

- ***Educate Yourself and Others***: Learn about the various sources of alpha-gal and educate family, friends, and caregivers about the importance of avoiding these triggers.

- *Plan Meals Carefully*: Prepare meals at home where you have full control over ingredients and preparation methods. Consider batch cooking and freezing safe meals for convenience.
- *Dining Out*: When eating out, choose restaurants that are willing to accommodate your dietary restrictions. Communicate clearly with restaurant staff about your allergy and inquire about their food preparation practices.
- *Carry Emergency Medications*: Always have an epinephrine auto-injector and antihistamines on hand in case of accidental exposure.
- *Join Support Groups*: Connect with others who have Alpha-Gal Allergy to share tips, recipes, and support.

Challenges and Strategies for Managing Alpha-Gal Allergy

Managing Alpha-Gal Allergy through avoidance can be challenging but is achievable with the right strategies:

- *Social Situations*: Navigating social events and gatherings can be difficult. Bring your own food to ensure you have safe options, and communicate your allergy to hosts beforehand.
- *Traveling*: When traveling, research food options and accommodations in advance. Pack non-perishable safe snacks and meals.

- *Hidden Sources*: Be aware of non-food sources of alpha-gal, such as certain medications, personal care products, and supplements. Consult with your healthcare provider to identify safe alternatives.

Avoiding known triggers is crucial for managing Alpha-Gal Allergy. By being careful with food labels, understanding cross-contamination risks, and employing practical strategies, individuals can greatly reduce their risk of allergic reactions. While managing this allergy can be tough, careful planning and proactive measures can lead to a safe and healthy life. Always consult a healthcare provider for personalized advice to ensure your management strategies meet your specific needs.

While natural remedies can help manage symptoms, they should not replace medical treatments, especially for severe allergic reactions. Always talk to a healthcare professional before starting any new treatment.

Managing Alpha-Gal Through Diet

Now that we have a better understanding of Alpha-Gal Allergy and its triggers, let's dive into the most critical aspect of managing this condition - diet. As mentioned earlier, avoiding foods and products derived from mammals is necessary to prevent allergic reactions in individuals with Alpha-Gal Allergy.

Foods to Avoid

Managing Alpha-Gal Allergy requires careful attention to dietary choices to avoid triggering allergic reactions. Here's a detailed overview of foods that should be avoided:

1. **Red Meats**

    Red meats from mammals are the primary culprits for triggering Alpha-Gal Allergy reactions. This includes:

    - *Beef*: Found in steaks, burgers, and many processed meat products.
    - *Pork*: Common in sausages, bacon, and ham.
    - *Lamb*: Often used in stews, roasts, and kebabs.
    - *Venison*: Popular in-game dishes.

- *Bison*: Sometimes used as a leaner alternative to beef.
- *Mutton and Goat*: Found in various ethnic cuisines.

These meats contain the alpha-gal molecule, which can cause allergic reactions ranging from mild symptoms like hives to severe anaphylaxis.

2. **Dairy Products**

Many individuals with Alpha-Gal Allergy also react to dairy products, as they come from mammals. Dairy items to avoid include:

- *Milk*: Both cow's milk and milk from other mammals.
- *Cheese*: All types, including hard and soft varieties.
- *Yogurt*: Both plain and flavored versions.
- *Butter and Cream*: Used in cooking and baking.

The presence of alpha-gal in these products can trigger allergic responses similar to those caused by mammalian meats.

3. **Processed Foods Containing Mammalian Meat or By-Products**

Processed foods often contain hidden sources of alpha-gal. Foods to be cautious about include:

- *Sausages and Hot Dogs*: Frequently made with a mix of meats and fillers.
- *Deli Meats*: These include salami, pepperoni, and bologna.
- *Gelatin*: Found in jellies, marshmallows, and some candies.
- *Broths and Stocks*: Especially those labeled as "beef" or "pork" broth.
- *Meat-Based Soups and Stews*: Often contain mammalian meat or stock.
- *Certain Baked Goods*: Like pastries and pies may use lard or gelatin.

4. **Hidden Sources of Alpha-Gal**

Alpha-gal can lurk in unexpected places, making it crucial to read labels carefully. Hidden sources include:

- *Gelatin*: Used as a gelling agent in many products, derived from animal bones and connective tissues.
- *Certain Medications*: Some capsules and tablets use gelatin-based coatings.

- ***Cosmetics and Personal Care Products***: Ingredients like lanolin, derived from sheep wool, can contain alpha-gal.
- ***Processed Foods***: Any food item with "natural flavors" or "natural ingredients" could potentially harbor mammalian by-products.
- ***Supplements***: Capsules and tablets may use gelatin or other animal-derived substances.

5. **Nuances and Specific Considerations**
   - ***Poultry and Fish***: Foods like chicken, turkey, and seafood are generally safe and do not contain alpha-gal. However, cross-contamination in cooking areas can pose a risk.
   - ***Plant-Based Alternatives***: Soy, nuts, seeds, and legumes are excellent protein sources and are safe for those with Alpha-Gal Allergy.
   - ***Check Labels***: Always scrutinize ingredient lists and inquire about food preparation methods when dining out. Even trace amounts of alpha-gal can cause reactions.

By avoiding these foods and being vigilant about hidden sources, individuals with Alpha-Gal Allergy can significantly reduce the risk of allergic reactions and lead a healthier, more comfortable life.

Foods to Eat

Navigating dietary choices with Alpha-Gal Allergy can be challenging, but numerous safe and nutritious options are available. Here's a detailed guide on foods you can enjoy:

1. **Safe Protein Sources**

   For those with Alpha-Gal Allergy, it's essential to find protein sources that do not contain the alpha-gal molecule. Safe options include:

   - *Poultry*: Chicken, turkey, and duck are excellent protein sources that are free from alpha-gal.
   - *Fish and Seafood*: Salmon, tuna, shrimp, and other seafood are safe and provide essential omega-3 fatty acids.
   - *Plant-Based Proteins*: Beans, lentils, chickpeas, tofu, tempeh, and edamame are rich in protein and fiber, making them great meat alternatives.
   - *Nuts and Seeds*: Almonds, walnuts, chia seeds, flaxseeds, and sunflower seeds offer protein, healthy fats, and vital nutrients.

2. **Fruits and Vegetables**

   Fruits and vegetables are naturally free of alpha-gal and should constitute a significant portion of your diet. They provide vitamins, minerals, and antioxidants:

- *Fruits*: Berries, apples, oranges, bananas, grapes, and melons are all safe and nutritious.
- *Vegetables*: Leafy greens (spinach, kale, lettuce), root vegetables (carrots, beets, sweet potatoes), and cruciferous vegetables (broccoli, cauliflower, Brussels sprouts) are excellent choices.

3. Grains and Cereals

Whole grains and cereals are also safe and provide essential nutrients, including fiber and B vitamins:

- *Whole Grains*: Brown rice, quinoa, oats, barley, and farro are excellent options.
- *Breads and Pastas*: Whole grain breads and pastas made without dairy or animal-derived ingredients are safe and nutritious.

4. Dairy Alternatives

Since dairy products contain alpha-gal, opt for plant-based alternatives:

- *Milk Alternatives*: Almond milk, soy milk, oat milk, and coconut milk are safe choices.
- *Plant-Based Yogurt*: Alternatives made from almond, soy, or coconut milk can replace traditional yogurt.
- *Non-Dairy Cheese*: Various plant-based cheeses made from nuts or soy are available.

5. **Other Safe Food Categories**
    - *Oils and Fats*: Olive oil, coconut oil, avocado oil, and other plant-based oils are safe for cooking and baking.
    - *Herbs and Spices*: Fresh and dried herbs (basil, cilantro, rosemary) and spices (turmeric, cumin, paprika) can enhance the flavor of your meals.
    - *Legumes and Pulses*: Lentils, chickpeas, black beans, and peas are versatile and protein-rich ingredients.

Nuances and Specific Considerations

- *Cross-Contamination*: Be cautious of cross-contamination, especially when dining out. Ensure that your food is prepared separately from mammalian meat and dairy products.
- *Plant-Based Benefits*: Embracing a plant-based diet can offer numerous health benefits, including reduced risk of chronic diseases and improved overall health.
- *Label Checking*: Always read labels carefully to ensure that no hidden animal-derived ingredients are present. Look for certifications like "vegan" or "plant-based" to be sure.

By focusing on these safe and nutritious foods, individuals with Alpha-Gal Allergy can enjoy a varied and satisfying diet while effectively managing their condition.

7-Day Sample Meal Plan

To help get you started on your plant-based journey with Alpha-Gal Allergy, here is a 7-day sample meal plan to give you an idea of what a week of meals could look like. This plan includes breakfast, lunch, dinner, and snacks for each day.

Day 1

- *Breakfast*: Overnight oats made with almond milk, topped with fresh berries and sliced almonds
- *Lunch*: Hummus and veggie wrap made with whole grain tortilla, hummus, lettuce, tomato, cucumber, and bell peppers
- *Dinner*: Lentil curry served over quinoa
- Snacks: Carrot sticks with homemade avocado dip

Day 2

- *Breakfast*: Tofu scramble with veggies and whole wheat toast
- *Lunch*: Black bean and corn salad with avocado served on a bed of mixed greens

- *Dinner*: Baked sweet potato topped with black beans, salsa, and guacamole
- *Snacks*: Apple slices with almond butter

Day 3

- *Breakfast*: Smoothie made with banana, spinach, almond milk, and chia seeds
- *Lunch*: Quinoa veggie bowl topped with tempeh and tahini dressing
- *Dinner*: Cauliflower steak served with roasted vegetables and brown rice
- *Snacks*: Homemade energy balls made with dates, oats, and peanut butter

Day 4

- *Breakfast*: Whole grain toast with mashed avocado and scrambled tofu
- *Lunch*: Lentil soup served with a side of whole-grain bread
- *Dinner*: Vegan lasagna made with zucchini noodles, tofu ricotta, and marinara sauce
- *Snacks*: Roasted chickpeas seasoned with spices of your choice

Day 5

- *Breakfast*: Chia pudding topped with fresh fruit and nuts

- *Lunch*: Brown rice sushi rolls filled with avocado, cucumber, and carrots
- *Dinner*: Stuffed bell peppers filled with quinoa, black beans, tomatoes, and corn
- *Snacks*: Celery sticks with almond butter and raisins on top (aka "ants on a log")

Day 6

- *Breakfast*: Oatmeal topped with almond milk, sliced banana, and a sprinkle of cinnamon
- *Lunch*: Veggie burger on whole wheat bun with tomato, lettuce, and avocado spread
- *Dinner*: Stir fry made with tofu, mixed vegetables, and brown rice
- *Snacks*: Homemade trail mix with dried fruit and nuts

Day 7

- *Breakfast*: Avocado toast topped with cherry tomatoes and balsamic glaze
- *Lunch*: Quinoa salad with roasted vegetables, chickpeas, and a lemon vinaigrette dressing
- *Dinner*: Vegan chili served over sweet potato noodles
- *Snacks*: Fresh fruit smoothie made with almond milk and protein powder

Tips for Making a Meal Plan

Creating a plant-based meal plan can seem overwhelming at first, but with some helpful tips and organization, it can become an easy and enjoyable task. Here are some tips to keep in mind when making your next meal plan:

1. ***Focus on Safe Foods***: Begin by understanding which foods contain alpha-gal and should be avoided, primarily mammalian products. Incorporate a variety of plant-based proteins, poultry, and fish to ensure nutritional balance.
2. ***Read Labels Meticulously***: Many processed foods contain hidden mammalian ingredients. Stick to whole, unprocessed foods whenever possible and familiarize yourself with different names that mammalian products might be listed under on ingredient labels.
3. ***Engage with Local Farmers' Markets***: Sourcing fresh produce from local farmers' markets can provide safer options. Build relationships with vendors and ask detailed questions about the origins and handling of their products.
4. ***Batch Cook and Meal Prep***: Prepare larger quantities of safe meals and freeze portions to have quick options on busy days, reducing the risk of accidental exposure to alpha-gal.
5. ***Create a List of Go-To Recipes***: Develop a collection of favorite recipes that are both delicious and safe.

Exploring different cuisines and trying new recipes can introduce variety and prevent the diet from becoming monotonous.

6. ***Maintain a Well-Stocked Pantry***: Keep a pantry filled with safe staples to ensure ingredients are always on hand for a quick, nutritious meal. Stock up on grains, legumes, and a variety of spices.
7. ***Plan for Dining Out***: Check restaurant menus in advance and call ahead to discuss dietary needs with the chef or manager. Develop a clear and concise way to communicate the allergy to restaurant staff.
8. ***Prepare for Travel***: Pack safe snacks and meals for journeys to provide peace of mind. Research restaurants and grocery stores at your destination beforehand to find safe food options.

By following these tips, individuals managing Alpha-Gal Allergy can enjoy diverse and satisfying meals while maintaining their health and well-being.

Sample Recipes

Now that you have a general idea of what a vegan meal plan could look like, here are some sample recipes to get you started:

Overnight Oats

Ingredients:

- 1 cup rolled oats
- 1 cup almond milk (unsweetened or sweetened, based on preference)
- 1 tablespoon chia seeds
- 1 teaspoon vanilla extract
- 1 tablespoon honey or maple syrup (optional)
- 1/2 cup fresh berries (strawberries, blueberries, raspberries, or a mix)
- 2 tablespoons sliced almonds
- A pinch of salt

Instructions:

1. Combine Ingredients: In a medium-sized bowl or a mason jar, combine the rolled oats, almond milk, chia seeds, vanilla extract, and honey or maple syrup if using. Add a pinch of salt to enhance the flavors.
2. Mix Well: Stir all the ingredients together until well combined. If using a mason jar, you can put the lid on and shake it to mix.
3. Refrigerate Overnight: Cover the bowl with plastic wrap or seal the mason jar with its lid. Place it in the

refrigerator and let it sit overnight, or for at least 4-5 hours, to allow the oats and chia seeds to absorb the liquid and soften.

4. Serve: In the morning, give the oats a good stir. Top with fresh berries and sliced almonds before serving.

Hummus and Veggie Wrap

Ingredients:

- 1 whole grain tortilla
- 1/4 cup hummus (store-bought or homemade)
- 1/2 cup lettuce, shredded
- 1 medium tomato, sliced
- 1/2 cucumber, sliced
- 1/2 bell pepper, sliced (any color)
- 1 tablespoon crumbled feta cheese (optional)
- Salt and pepper to taste

Instructions:

1. Prepare Veggies: Wash and slice the lettuce, tomato, cucumber, and bell pepper.
2. Spread Hummus: Lay the whole-grain tortilla flat on a clean surface. Spread the hummus evenly over the tortilla, leaving about 1 inch around the edges.
3. Add Veggies: Arrange the shredded lettuce, tomato slices, cucumber slices, and bell pepper slices over the hummus.
4. Season: Sprinkle with salt and pepper to taste. Add crumbled feta cheese if using.

5. Wrap It Up: Carefully roll the tortilla tightly, tucking in the sides as you go, to form a wrap.
6. Slice and Serve: Slice the wrap in half diagonally and serve immediately, or wrap it in parchment paper for an on-the-go meal.

Lentil Curry Over Quinoa

Ingredients:

For the Lentil Curry:

- 1 cup green or brown lentils, rinsed and drained
- 1 tablespoon olive oil
- 1 medium onion, chopped
- 2 cloves garlic, minced
- 1-inch piece of ginger, minced
- 1 can (14.5 oz) diced tomatoes
- 1 can (14 oz) coconut milk
- 2 cups vegetable broth or water
- 1 tablespoon curry powder
- 1 teaspoon ground cumin
- 1 teaspoon ground coriander
- 1/2 teaspoon turmeric
- 1/4 teaspoon cayenne pepper (optional, for heat)
- Salt and pepper to taste
- Fresh cilantro, chopped (for garnish)

For the Quinoa:

- 1 cup quinoa
- 2 cups water or vegetable broth
- A pinch of salt

Instructions:

Cook the Quinoa:

1. Rinse the quinoa under cold water.
2. In a medium saucepan, bring 2 cups of water or vegetable broth to a boil. Add a pinch of salt.
3. Stir in the quinoa, reduce the heat to low, cover, and simmer for about 15 minutes, or until the water is absorbed and the quinoa is tender.
4. Fluff with a fork and set aside.

Prepare the Lentil Curry:

5. In a large pot or Dutch oven, heat the olive oil over medium heat.
6. Add the chopped onion and sauté until translucent, about 5 minutes.
7. Add the minced garlic and ginger, and sauté for an additional 1-2 minutes until fragrant.
8. Stir in the curry powder, ground cumin, ground coriander, turmeric, and cayenne pepper (if using). Cook for 1 minute to toast the spices.
9. Add the lentils, diced tomatoes (with their juice), coconut milk, and vegetable broth. Stir to combine.
10. Bring to a boil, then reduce the heat to low and simmer, uncovered, for about 25-30 minutes, or until the lentils are tender and the curry has thickened. Stir occasionally to prevent sticking.
11. Season with salt and pepper to taste.

Serve:

12. Spoon the cooked quinoa into bowls.
13. Ladle the lentil curry over the quinoa.
14. Garnish with fresh cilantro.

Tofu Scramble with Veggies and Whole Wheat Toast

Ingredients:

- 1 block firm tofu, drained and crumbled
- 1 tablespoon olive oil
- 1 small onion, chopped
- 1 bell pepper, chopped (any color)
- 1 cup baby spinach
- 1 clove garlic, minced
- 1/2 teaspoon turmeric
- 1/2 teaspoon ground cumin
- Salt and pepper to taste
- 2 slices whole wheat bread
- Optional: nutritional yeast, for a cheesy flavor

Instructions:

1. Prepare Tofu: Drain the tofu and crumble it into small pieces using your hands or a fork.
2. Cook Veggies: Heat the olive oil in a large skillet over medium heat. Add the chopped onion and bell pepper, and sauté for about 5 minutes, or until softened.
3. Add Garlic: Add the minced garlic and cook for another minute until fragrant.
4. Add Tofu and Spices: Stir in the crumbled tofu, turmeric, ground cumin, salt, and pepper. Cook for

about 5-7 minutes, stirring occasionally, until the tofu is heated through and slightly browned.
5. Add Spinach: Add the baby spinach and cook for another 1-2 minutes until wilted. If using nutritional yeast, sprinkle it over the tofu scramble and stir to combine.
6. Toast Bread: While the tofu scramble is cooking, toast the whole wheat bread slices to your desired level of crispiness.
7. Serve: Serve the tofu scramble hot alongside the whole wheat toast.

Black Bean and Corn Salad with Avocado on Mixed Greens

Ingredients:

- 1 can (15 oz) black beans, rinsed and drained
- 1 cup corn kernels (fresh, frozen, or canned)
- 1 avocado, diced
- 1 red bell pepper, chopped
- 1/4 red onion, finely chopped
- 1/4 cup fresh cilantro, chopped
- 1 tablespoon olive oil
- 1 lime, juiced
- Salt and pepper to taste
- Mixed greens (arugula, spinach, or your choice)

Instructions:

1. Prepare Salad: In a large bowl, combine the black beans, corn, diced avocado, chopped red bell pepper, and finely chopped red onion.
2. Add Cilantro: Stir in the chopped fresh cilantro.
3. Dress Salad: Drizzle the olive oil and lime juice over the salad. Toss gently to combine.
4. Season: Season with salt and pepper to taste.
5. Serve: Arrange the mixed greens on a serving plate or in a bowl. Top with the black bean and corn salad. Serve immediately.

Baked Sweet Potato Topped

Ingredients:

- 2 large sweet potatoes
- 1 can (15 oz) black beans, rinsed and drained
- 1 cup salsa (store-bought or homemade)
- 1 avocado
- 1 lime, juiced
- Salt and pepper to taste
- Optional: fresh cilantro, chopped, for garnish

Instructions:

Bake Sweet Potatoes:

1. Preheat the oven to 400°F (200°C).
2. Wash and scrub the sweet potatoes. Pierce them several times with a fork.
3. Place on a baking sheet and bake for 45-60 minutes, or until tender when pierced with a fork.

Prepare Guacamole:

4. While the sweet potatoes are baking, make the guacamole. Mash the avocado in a bowl and stir in lime juice, salt, and pepper to taste.
5. Heat Black Beans: In a small saucepan, heat the black beans over medium heat until warmed through.

Assemble:

6. Once the sweet potatoes are done, let them cool slightly. Cut them open lengthwise and fluff the insides with a fork.
7. Top each sweet potato with a generous scoop of black beans.
8. Add salsa and a dollop of guacamole on top.
9. Garnish with fresh cilantro if desired.
10. Serve: Serve the baked sweet potatoes hot, with additional salsa and guacamole on the side if desired.

Smoothie Made with Banana, Spinach, Almond Milk, and Chia Seeds

Ingredients:

- 1 banana, peeled
- 1 cup fresh spinach leaves, washed
- 1 cup almond milk (unsweetened or sweetened based on preference)
- 1 tablespoon chia seeds
- 1/2 cup ice cubes (optional, for a thicker smoothie)
- 1 teaspoon honey or maple syrup (optional, for added sweetness)

Instructions:

1. Blend Ingredients: In a blender, combine the banana, fresh spinach leaves, almond milk, chia seeds, and ice cubes if using.
2. Add Sweetener: Add honey or maple syrup if you prefer a sweeter smoothie.
3. Blend Until Smooth: Blend on high speed until the mixture is smooth and creamy, with no visible pieces of spinach. This should take about 1-2 minutes.
4. Serve Immediately: Pour the smoothie into a glass and serve immediately.

Quinoa Veggie Bowl Topped with Tempeh and Tahini Dressing

Ingredients:

For the Quinoa Veggie Bowl:

- 1 cup quinoa, rinsed
- 2 cups water or vegetable broth
- 1 cup cherry tomatoes, halved
- 1 cucumber, diced
- 1 red bell pepper, chopped
- 1/2 cup shredded carrots
- 1 avocado, sliced
- 1 block tempeh, cubed
- 1 tablespoon olive oil
- Salt and pepper to taste

For the Tahini Dressing:

- 1/4 cup tahini
- 2 tablespoons lemon juice
- 1 garlic clove, minced
- 2-3 tablespoons water (to thin)
- Salt to taste

Instructions:

Cook Quinoa:

1. In a medium saucepan, bring 2 cups of water or vegetable broth to a boil. Add a pinch of salt.
2. Stir in the rinsed quinoa, reduce the heat to low, cover, and simmer for about 15 minutes or until the liquid is absorbed and the quinoa is tender.
3. Fluff with a fork and set aside.

Prepare Tempeh:

4. In a skillet, heat 1 tablespoon of olive oil over medium heat.
5. Add the cubed tempeh and cook until golden brown on all sides, about 5-7 minutes.
6. Season with salt and pepper to taste.

Prepare Vegetables:

7. Wash and chop the cherry tomatoes, cucumber, red bell pepper, and shred the carrots.
8. Slice the avocado.

Make Tahini Dressing:

9. In a small bowl, whisk together the tahini, lemon juice, minced garlic, and salt.
10. Gradually add water, one tablespoon at a time, until the dressing reaches your desired consistency.

Assemble the Bowl:

11. In a large bowl, layer the cooked quinoa, cherry tomatoes, cucumber, red bell pepper, shredded carrots, and sliced avocado.
12. Top with the golden brown tempeh cubes.
13. Drizzle the tahini dressing over the bowl.

Serve:

14. Serve immediately, or refrigerate for up to 2 days for a convenient meal-prep option.

Cauliflower Steak with Roasted Vegetables and Brown Rice

Ingredients:

For the Cauliflower Steak:

- 1 large cauliflower head, cut into 1-inch thick slices
- 2 tablespoons olive oil
- 1 teaspoon paprika
- 1/2 teaspoon garlic powder
- Salt and pepper to taste

For the Roasted Vegetables:

- 1 zucchini, sliced
- 1 red bell pepper, chopped
- 1 red onion, sliced
- 1 tablespoon olive oil
- Salt and pepper to taste

For the Brown Rice:

- 1 cup brown rice
- 2 cups water or vegetable broth
- A pinch of salt

Instructions:

Prepare Brown Rice:

1. In a medium saucepan, bring 2 cups of water or vegetable broth to a boil. Add a pinch of salt.
2. Add the brown rice, reduce the heat to low, cover, and simmer for about 40-45 minutes, or until the rice is tender and the liquid is absorbed.
3. Fluff with a fork and set aside.

Prepare Cauliflower Steaks:

4. Preheat the oven to 425°F (220°C).
5. Slice the cauliflower head into 1-inch thick steaks. Place them on a baking sheet lined with parchment paper.
6. Brush both sides of the cauliflower steaks with olive oil. Sprinkle with paprika, garlic powder, salt, and pepper.
7. Roast in the oven for 25-30 minutes, flipping halfway through, until the cauliflower is golden brown and tender.

Prepare Roasted Vegetables:

8. In a mixing bowl, toss the sliced zucchini, chopped red bell pepper, and sliced red onion with olive oil, salt, and pepper.
9. Spread the vegetables on another baking sheet lined with parchment paper.

10. Roast in the oven for 20-25 minutes, stirring once halfway through, until the vegetables are tender and slightly caramelized.

Assemble the Plate:

11. On a plate, place a serving of brown rice.
12. Add a roasted cauliflower steak on top of the rice.
13. Arrange the roasted vegetables around the cauliflower steak.

Serve:

14. Serve immediately, garnished with fresh herbs like parsley or cilantro if desired.

Oatmeal Topped with Almond Milk, Sliced Banana, and a Sprinkle of Cinnamon

Ingredients:

- 1 cup rolled oats
- 2 cups almond milk (unsweetened or sweetened based on preference)
- 1 ripe banana, sliced
- 1/2 teaspoon ground cinnamon
- Optional: Honey or maple syrup, for added sweetness

Instructions:

Cook Oats:

1. In a medium saucepan, bring the almond milk to a gentle boil over medium heat.
2. Stir in the rolled oats and reduce the heat to low. Simmer for about 5-7 minutes, stirring occasionally, until the oats are tender and the mixture has thickened.

Serve:

3. Spoon the cooked oatmeal into a bowl.
4. Top with sliced banana and a sprinkle of ground cinnamon.

5. Drizzle with honey or maple syrup if you prefer additional sweetness.

Enjoy Immediately:

6. Serve hot, with an extra splash of almond milk if desired.

Veggie Burger on Whole Wheat Bun with Tomato, Lettuce, and Avocado Spread

Ingredients:

- 4 veggie burger patties (store-bought or homemade)
- 4 whole wheat buns
- 1 large tomato, sliced
- 4 lettuce leaves
- 1 ripe avocado
- 1 tablespoon lemon juice
- Salt and pepper to taste
- Optional: pickles, red onion slices, or any other preferred toppings

Instructions:

Prepare Avocado Spread:

1. In a small bowl, mash the ripe avocado with a fork until smooth.
2. Stir in the lemon juice, and season with salt and pepper to taste. Set aside.

Cook Veggie Burgers:

3. Cook the veggie burger patties according to the package instructions or your homemade recipe. This can typically be done by grilling, baking, or pan-frying until heated through and lightly browned.

Assemble Burgers:

4. Lightly toast the whole wheat buns if desired.
5. Spread a generous amount of avocado spread on the bottom half of each bun.
6. Place a cooked veggie burger patty on top of the avocado spread.
7. Add a slice of tomato and a lettuce leaf.
8. Cover with the top half of the bun.

Serve:

9. Serve immediately with your favorite sides, such as a salad or sweet potato fries.

Stir Fry Made with Tofu, Mixed Vegetables, and Brown Rice

Ingredients:

- 1 block of firm tofu, drained and cubed
- 2 tablespoons soy sauce (or tamari for gluten-free)
- 1 tablespoon cornstarch
- 2 tablespoons vegetable oil
- 1 onion, sliced
- 2 bell peppers, sliced
- 1 cup broccoli florets
- 1 cup snap peas
- 2 carrots, julienned
- 2 cloves garlic, minced
- 1 tablespoon ginger, minced
- 3 cups cooked brown rice
- Optional: sesame seeds, for garnish

Instructions:

Prepare Tofu:

1. In a bowl, toss the cubed tofu with soy sauce and cornstarch until evenly coated.
2. Heat 1 tablespoon of vegetable oil in a large skillet or wok over medium-high heat. Add the tofu and cook until golden brown and crispy on all sides, about 5-7 minutes. Remove tofu from the skillet and set aside.

Cook Vegetables:

3. In the same skillet, add the remaining tablespoon of vegetable oil.
4. Add the sliced onion, bell peppers, broccoli, snap peas, and carrots. Stir-fry for about 5-7 minutes, or until the vegetables are tender-crisp.

Add Aromatics:

5. Stir in the minced garlic and ginger. Cook for an additional 1-2 minutes until fragrant.

Combine Tofu and Vegetables:

6. Return the cooked tofu to the skillet and toss to combine with the vegetables.
7. Add additional soy sauce to taste, if desired.

Serve:

8. Serve the tofu and vegetable stir-fry over a bed of cooked brown rice.
9. Garnish with sesame seeds if desired.

Avocado Toast Topped with Cherry Tomatoes and Balsamic Glaze

Ingredients:

- 2 slices whole grain bread
- 1 ripe avocado, peeled and pitted
- 1 tablespoon lemon juice
- Salt and pepper to taste
- 1 cup cherry tomatoes, halved
- Balsamic glaze, for drizzling
- Optional: red pepper flakes, for a spicy kick

Instructions:

Prepare Avocado:

1. In a small bowl, mash the avocado with a fork until smooth.
2. Stir in the lemon juice and season with salt and pepper to taste.

Toast-Bread:

3. Toast the whole-grain bread slices to your desired level of crispiness.

Assemble Toast:

4. Spread the mashed avocado evenly over the toasted bread slices.
5. Top with halved cherry tomatoes.

Drizzle with Balsamic Glaze:

6. Drizzle balsamic glaze over the avocado and cherry tomatoes.
7. Optionally, sprinkle with red pepper flakes for a spicy kick.

Serve:

8. Serve immediately and enjoy.

Quinoa Salad with Roasted Vegetables, Chickpeas, and a Lemon Vinaigrette Dressing

Ingredients:

- 1 cup quinoa, rinsed
- 2 cups water or vegetable broth
- 1 can (15 oz) chickpeas, rinsed and drained
- 1 red bell pepper, chopped
- 1 zucchini, chopped
- 1 cup cherry tomatoes, halved
- 1/2 red onion, chopped
- 1 tablespoon olive oil
- Salt and pepper to taste
- Fresh parsley, chopped (for garnish)

For the Lemon Vinaigrette:

- 1/4 cup olive oil
- 2 tablespoons lemon juice
- 1 teaspoon Dijon mustard
- 1 clove garlic, minced
- Salt and pepper to taste

Instructions:

Cook Quinoa:

1. In a medium saucepan, bring water or vegetable broth to a boil.
2. Add quinoa, reduce the heat to low, cover, and simmer for about 15 minutes, or until the liquid is absorbed and the quinoa is tender.
3. Fluff with a fork and set aside to cool.

Roast Vegetables:

4. Preheat the oven to 400°F (200°C).
5. On a baking sheet, toss the chopped bell pepper, zucchini, cherry tomatoes, and red onion with olive oil, salt, and pepper.
6. Roast for about 20-25 minutes, or until the vegetables are tender and slightly charred.

Prepare Lemon Vinaigrette:

7. In a small bowl, whisk together olive oil, lemon juice, Dijon mustard, minced garlic, salt, and pepper until well combined.

Assemble Salad:

8. In a large bowl, combine the cooked quinoa, roasted vegetables, and chickpeas.

9. Drizzle with lemon vinaigrette dressing and toss to coat evenly.
10. Garnish with chopped fresh parsley.

Serve:

11. Serve chilled or at room temperature.

Vegan Chili Served Over Sweet Potato Noodles

Ingredients:

- 1 tablespoon olive oil
- 1 large onion, chopped
- 2 cloves garlic, minced
- 1 red bell pepper, chopped
- 1 green bell pepper, chopped
- 1 can (15 oz) black beans, rinsed and drained
- 1 can (15 oz) kidney beans, rinsed and drained
- 1 can (28 oz) crushed tomatoes
- 2 tablespoons tomato paste
- 1 cup vegetable broth
- 1 tablespoon chili powder
- 1 teaspoon ground cumin
- 1 teaspoon smoked paprika
- Salt and pepper to taste
- 3 large sweet potatoes, spiralized into noodles
- Fresh cilantro, chopped (for garnish)
- Optional: avocado slices, for topping

Instructions:

Prepare Chili:

1. In a large pot, heat olive oil over medium heat.
2. Add the chopped onion and sauté until translucent, about 5 minutes.

3. Stir in the minced garlic and cook for another minute until fragrant.
4. Add the chopped bell peppers and cook for about 5 minutes until softened.
5. Stir in the black beans, kidney beans, crushed tomatoes, tomato paste, and vegetable broth.
6. Add chili powder, ground cumin, smoked paprika, salt, and pepper. Stir well to combine.
7. Bring the mixture to a boil, then reduce the heat to low and simmer for about 30 minutes, stirring occasionally.

Prepare Sweet Potato Noodles:

8. While the chili is simmering, bring a large pot of water to a boil.
9. Add the spiralized sweet potato noodles and cook for about 3-4 minutes until tender but still firm.
10. Drain the noodles and set aside.

Serve:

11. To serve, place a portion of sweet potato noodles in a bowl.
12. Ladle the vegan chili over the noodles.
13. Garnish with chopped fresh cilantro and optional avocado slices

Conclusion

Thank you for taking the time to read through the Alpha-Gal Allergy Management Guide. Reaching the end of this comprehensive resource signifies your commitment to understanding and managing your condition effectively. Your dedication to learning about Alpha Gal Syndrome and its implications is commendable, and it's a significant step toward reclaiming control over your health and well-being.

Living with Alpha-Gal Allergy can be challenging, but it's important to remember that you are not alone on this journey. By educating yourself, you have equipped yourself with the knowledge needed to navigate this condition with confidence. The road ahead may have its ups and downs, but with the right strategies in place, you can lead a full and satisfying life despite the restrictions imposed by this allergy.

Managing an Alpha-Gal Allergy requires vigilance and adaptability. You've learned about the importance of reading labels meticulously, understanding cross-contamination risks, and knowing which foods and products to avoid. This newfound awareness empowers you to make informed choices that protect your health. It's a continuous learning process, but each decision you make brings you closer to a safer and more comfortable lifestyle.

Adapting to a new diet and lifestyle can be overwhelming at first, but it's also an opportunity to explore new foods and recipes that you may not have considered before. Embrace this chance to discover delicious plant-based meals, creative meat substitutes, and other alternatives that align with your dietary needs. Over time, you will build a repertoire of go-to dishes that not only satisfy your taste buds but also keep you safe from allergic reactions.

One of the most valuable insights from this guide is the importance of communicating openly with those around you. Friends, family, and coworkers can provide crucial support when they understand the nature of your allergy and the precautions you must take. Don't hesitate to educate them about Alpha Gal Syndrome and how they can help you avoid potential triggers. Clear communication fosters a supportive environment where everyone is aware of and respects your dietary restrictions.

Your healthcare team is another vital resource in your management plan. Regular consultations with your allergist or physician ensure that you stay on top of your condition and any new developments. They can also offer personalized advice and adjustments to your management plan as needed.

Keep an open line of communication with them and don't hesitate to ask questions or express concerns.

Living with Alpha-Gal Allergy also means being prepared for emergencies. You've learned about the importance of carrying an epinephrine auto-injector and knowing how to use it. This preparedness can be lifesaving in the event of an accidental exposure. Make sure that those close to you know where you keep your auto-injector and how to administer it if necessary. Practicing these emergency procedures can provide peace of mind and ensure that you are ready to act swiftly if the situation arises.

Your journey with Alpha-Gal Allergy is a testament to your resilience and adaptability. Each challenge you face is an opportunity to grow stronger and more knowledgeable about your condition. The insights and strategies you've gained from this guide will serve as your foundation, but remember that you are always learning and evolving. Stay curious, stay informed, and stay proactive in your approach to managing your allergy.

In the face of dietary restrictions, it's easy to feel limited, but focusing on what you can enjoy rather than what you must avoid can shift your perspective. Celebrate the foods that make you feel good and nourish your body. Explore new cuisines, experiment with different ingredients, and find joy in the culinary journey. Your positive attitude and willingness to adapt will make a significant difference in how you experience life with Alpha-Gal Allergy.

Thank you once again for dedicating your time to this guide. Your proactive approach and willingness to learn are commendable and will serve you well as you navigate the complexities of Alpha-Gal Syndrome. Remember, you have the knowledge, tools, and support needed to manage your allergy effectively.

FAQs

What are the common symptoms of Alpha-Gal Allergy?

Common symptoms of Alpha-Gal Allergy can include hives, itching, swelling, stomach pain, diarrhea, nausea, and in severe cases, anaphylaxis. Symptoms typically appear 3-6 hours after consuming mammalian meat products, unlike most food allergies, which cause reactions within minutes.

What foods and products should I avoid if I have Alpha-Gal Allergy?

If you have Alpha-Gal Allergy, you should avoid all mammalian meat products, including beef, pork, lamb, venison, and other red meats. Additionally, be cautious with products containing gelatin, dairy, and certain medications or supplements that might be derived from mammalian sources.

How can I prevent cross-contamination when preparing meals?

To prevent cross-contamination, use separate utensils, cutting boards, and cookware for allergen-free foods. Thoroughly clean surfaces and wash hands after handling mammalian meat products. Educate family and friends about the importance of preventing cross-contamination to help you stay safe.

What are some safe and delicious alternatives to red meat?

Safe and delicious alternatives to red meat include poultry, fish, plant-based proteins like tofu and tempeh, legumes, and various meat substitutes made from soy, peas, or other non-mammalian sources. Experimenting with these options can help you find satisfying and nutritious meals.

Why is it important to communicate my allergy to others?

Communicating your allergy to friends, family, coworkers, and food service providers is crucial for your safety. Educating them about your condition and the necessary precautions helps create a supportive environment where everyone is aware of and respects your dietary restrictions.

How should I prepare for an emergency allergic reaction?

Always carry an epinephrine auto-injector and ensure you and those around you know how to use it. Inform close contacts about where you keep your auto-injector and the signs of an allergic reaction. Practicing emergency procedures can provide peace of mind and readiness in case of accidental exposure.

How often should I see my healthcare provider for Alpha-Gal Allergy management?

Regular consultations with your allergist or physician are essential for monitoring your condition and staying updated on any new developments. Your healthcare provider can offer personalized advice, adjust your management plan as needed, and address any questions or concerns you might have.

References and Helpful Links

Alpha-Gal Syndrome (AGS). (2023, October 5). Yale Medicine. https://www.yalemedicine.org/conditions/alpha-gal-syndrome-ags#:~:text=Treatments%20for%20allergic%20reactions%20caused,case%20of%20an%20allergic%20reaction.

Alpha-gal syndrome: How a tick bite can make you allergic to meat | Prevention | UT Southwestern Medical Center. (n.d.). https://utswmed.org/medblog/meat-allergy-alpha-gal-tick-bite/

Alpha-gal and red meat allergy. (n.d.). https://www.aaaai.org/tools-for-the-public/conditions-library/allergies/alpha-gal-and-red-meat-allergy

Watson, K. (2019, January 30). Alpha-Gal allergy. Healthline. https://www.healthline.com/health/allergies/alpha-gal

Steinke, J. W., Platts-Mills, T. a. E., & Commins, S. P. (2015). The alpha-gal story: Lessons learned from connecting the dots. Journal of Allergy and Clinical Immunology, 135(3), 589–596. https://doi.org/10.1016/j.jaci.2014.12.1947

Alpha-Gal (Allergy) Arkansas Department of Health. (n.d.). https://www.healthy.arkansas.gov/programs-services/topics/alpha-gal-allergy

Scott, S. (2024, June 29). Alpha Gal Diet: What's Safe, Off-Limits, and Risky. Sage Alpha Gal. https://sagealphagal.com/alpha-gal-diet-whats-safe-off-limits-and-risky/

Palinski-Wade, E. (2023, August 5). The Alpha-Gal Allergy Diet: What you can eat with a red meat allergy? Erin Palinski-Wade. https://erinpalinski.com/alpha-gal-diet/

Alpha-Gal Cooking. (2018, February 9). Alpha-Gal Cooking. https://alphagalcooking.com/page/2/

Alpha Gal Allergy Cookbook: Healthy and Flavorful Recip. . . (n.d.). Goodreads. https://www.goodreads.com/book/show/60059197-alpha-gal-allergy-cookbook

www.ingramcontent.com/pod-product-compliance
Lightning Source LLC
LaVergne TN
LVHW010404070526
838199LV00065B/5891